THE STANDARD REUNIFICATION METHOD

SRM V2

REUNIFY

A Practical Method to Unite Students with Parents After an Evacuation or Crisis.
The "I Love U Guys" Foundation

SRM Version 2.1

PEACE

It does not mean to be in a place where there is no noise, trouble, or hard work.

It means to be in the midst of those things and still be calm in your heart.

STANDARD™ REUNIFICATION METHOD

CHANGE HISTORY VERSION 2.0

AUTHOR/CONTRIBUTOR	VERSION	REVISION DATE	REVISION COMMENTARY
John-Michael Keyes	0.9.0	09/17/2011	Preliminary Draft
John-Michael Keyes	0.9.1	10/01/2011	First Final Content Revision
Ellen Stoddard-Keyes	0.9.2	10/16/2011	Preliminary Edits
Lee Shaughnessy	0.9.3	10/26/2011	Preliminary Edits
Joseph Majsak. SVP & Chief Marketing Officer, Genesis Mgmt. & Ins. Services Corp.	1.0	11/16/2011	Continuity and Final Edits
John-Michael Keyes	1.1	06/08/2016	Additional Content
John-Michael Keyes, Will Schwall, Michelle Brady, Russ Deffner, Carolyn Mears	2.0	03/02/2017	Reunifier replaces Runner Additional Content Edits
John-Michael Keyes	2.1	03/27/2022	Changed Lockout to Secure

COMMITMENT

There are several things we are committed to. The most important thing we can do is offer our material at no cost to schools, districts, departments, agencies and organizations. The reason we are able to continue to provide this service is due, in part, to the generosity of our donors. The "I Love U Guys" Foundation works very hard to keep our costs down as well as any costs associated with our printed materials. Donor support allows us to stretch those dollars and services even more. Your gift, no matter the size, helps us achieve our mission.

Please visit www.iloveuguys.org and donate now. Your help makes a difference to our students, teachers, first responders, and the communities in which we live and work.

A Practical Method to Unite Students with Parents After an Evacuation or Crisis

The "I Love U Guys" Foundation

Version 2.0

ISBN-13: 978-1544013831
ISBN-10: 1544013833

THE "I LOVE U GUYS" FOUNDATION

On September 27th, 2006 a gunman entered Platte Canyon High School in Bailey, Colorado, held seven girls hostage and ultimately shot and killed Emily Keyes. During the time she was held hostage, Emily sent her parents text messages... "I love you guys" and "I love u guys. k?"

Emily's kindness, spirit, fierce joy, and the dignity and grace that followed this tragic event define the core of The "I Love U Guys" Foundation.

MISSION

The "I Love U Guys" Foundation was created to restore and protect the joy of youth through educational programs and positive actions in collaboration with families, schools, communities, organizations and government entities.

TERMS OF USE

Schools, districts, departments, agencies and organizations may use these materials, at no cost, under the following conditions:

1. Materials are not re-sold.
2. Notification of use is provided to The "I Love U Guys" Foundation through one of the following:
   2.1. Email notice of use to srm@iloveuguys.org
   2.2. Notice of Intent
   2.3. Memorandum of Understanding
3. The following modification to the materials (handouts, cards) are allowable:
   3.1. Localization

The "I Love U Guys" Foundation is committed to providing its programs at no cost to a widening variety of organizations.

To assess the fidelity of implementation within an organization, The Foundation has developed a certification program for the Standard Reunification Method (SRM). The certification program is optional and is not required to use the SRM within your organization.

COPYRIGHTS AND TRADEMARKS

In order to protect the integrity and consistency of the Standard Reunification Method, The "I Love U Guys" Foundation exercises all protection under copyright and trademark. Use of this material is governed by the Terms of Use.

WARNINGS AND DISCLAIMER

Every effort has been made to make this book as complete and accurate as possible, but no warranty or fitness is implied. The information provided is on an "as is" basis.

WHAT'S NEW IN THIS VERSION

There's tons of new stuff, but the only change in language is that the term *Reunifier* replaces *Runner*. Feedback from Emergency Managers encouraged the change.

AUTHOR/CONTRIBUTOR INFORMATION

John-Michael Keyes - Primary Author
The "I Love U Guys" Foundation
Executive Director

Russell Deffner - Contributing Author
The "I Love U Guys" Foundation
Advisor/Contractor/Volunteer

SPECIAL THANKS

Pat Hamilton – Executive Director of Operations, Adams 12 Five Star Schools, Colorado

Jeff Genger – Director of Emergency Management, Adams 12 Five Star Schools, Colorado

John McDonald – Executive Director, Safety, Security and Emergency Planning, Jefferson County Public Schools, Colorado

Will Schwall – Emergency Manager, Hays County Sheriff's Office, San Marcos, Texas

Michelle Brady – Emergency Planning Coordinator, Hillsboro School District, Oregon

Heidi Walts – Sergeant, Broomfield Police, Colorado

SRM REVIEW COMMITTEE

Pat Hamilton – Executive Director of Operations, Adams 12 Five Star Schools, Adams County, Colorado

Kevin Burd – Lieutenant, Hunterdon County Prosecutor's Office, New Jersey

Joseph Majsak – Senior Vice President & Chief Marketing Officer, Genesis Management & Insurance Services Corporation, Stamford, Connecticut

Kevin Griger – Captain, Sarpy County Sheriff's Office, Nebraska

CONTACT INFORMATION

The "I Love U Guys" Foundation can be reached online at http://iloveuguys.org.

Email: srm@iloveuguys.org.

The "I Love U Guys" Foundation
PO Box 1230
Bailey, CO 80421
303.426.3100

Executive Director
John-Michael Keyes
johnmichael@iloveuguys.org

Development Director
Sabra Jewell
sabra@iloveuguys.org

Operations Director
Ellen Stoddard-Keyes
ellen@iloveuguys.org

Project Coordinator
Elvira Beck
elvira@iloveuguys.org

"Recovery starts when the crisis begins."

"Reunification is the first step in the recovery process."
– John McDonald, Executive Director of Safety and Emergency Planning, Jeffco R1, Colorado

TABLE OF CONTENTS

"Tactics are intel driven."

What we plan is based on what we know.

"But the environment dictates tactics."

But what we do, is based on where we are.

– Sergeant A.J. DeAndrea
– Civilian Translation: John-Michael Keyes

STANDARD™ REUNIFICATION METHOD

ABOUT THIS BOOK

In 2012, The "I Love U Guys" Foundation introduced the Standard Reunification Method. At the time, we saw a void in school safety planning regarding student/parent reunification after a crisis. We were certain this was a true need, but few schools or districts actually had reunification plans and practices in place. Fewer still had actually drilled or practiced.

Was it truly a need? The answer lies in the widespread adoption of the SRM. Since 2012, thousands of schools in the US and Canada have implemented the Standard Reunification Method as a means to safely reunite students and families after a crisis.

Recovery starts when the crisis begins. Reunification is the first step in that recovery.

This is Version 2.0 of the Standard Reunification Method. But notice, we use the word *method*. Not *protocol*. Not *procedure*. Method.

What that means is that we provide you with some tactics. Things we know. But the event, your reunification site, your environment, will ultimately dictate what you do.

Please, in your planning, if you see something here that doesn't seem to work in your environment, figure out what does. Let us know.

"Cops own the crime. Fire owns the flames. Schools own the kids."

"But Paramedics own the patient."
And that may be an area of conflict during an event.
Your reunification plans and methods must be
communicated with first responders prior to a crisis.

REUNIFICATION

The nation has experienced high profile acts of school violence. In response to this and the everyday types of crisis, The "I Love U Guys" Foundation develops programs to help districts, departments and agencies respond to incidents.

One critical aspect of crisis response is accountable reunification of students with their parents or guardians in the event a controlled release is necessary. The Standard Reunification Method provides school and district safety

teams proven methods for planning, practicing and achieving a successful reunification. Keep in mind though, this is an evolving process. While there is a smattering of science in these methods, there is certainly more art. Site-specific considerations will impact how these practices can be integrated into school and district safety plans. Successful planning and implementation will also demand partnerships with all responding agencies participating in a crisis response.

WHY BOTHER?

Crisis recovery starts with the crisis, not after. Simply "winging it" when reuniting ignores not only the mental health demands that accompany a crisis, but the responsibility of the school and the district to maintain the chain of custody for every student.

No school is immune to stuff hitting the proverbial fan. Wildland or structural fires, hazardous materials, floods, tornados, blizzards, power outages, tsunamis, bomb threats, acts of violence, acts of terror... these just start the list of events that may necessitate a controlled reunification and release for a school or district.

A predetermined, practiced reunification method ensures the reunification process will not further complicate what is probably already a chaotic, anxiety-filled scene. In fact, putting an orderly reunification plan into action will help defuse emotion escalating at the site.

There is a hidden side effect of implementing the Standard Reunification Method. Going through the planning and training process may help strengthen district relationships with first responders. Often law enforcement is very active in partnering with schools and districts. Less often is the fire department. The SRM may be a vector into strengthening relationships with fire agencies as well.

WHAT DOES IT COST?

Implementing the Standard Reunification Method concepts and planning stages take a certain amount of time. But in the grand scheme of school safety, the level of effort is modest. There will be some staff hours committed to the planning, training and practice of these concepts. There will be some cost in printing and in creating the "go kits" necessary for a successful reunification. Since some of this activity is happening at the district level, the cost of "go kits" can be spread among all of the schools in the district.

ADAMS 12, FIVE STAR SCHOOLS METHOD

The core concept of the Adams 12 Reunification Method rests on accountability achieved through a process based on managing the physical location of students, staff and of incoming parents. The process also uses perforated cards. These cards are completed by parents or guardians at the reunification site. The cards are separated at the perforation, and a reunifier retrieves the child.

The methods detailed in the first version of the Standard Reunification Method are based on the practices developed at the Adams 12, Five Star School District, Thornton, Colorado, by Pat Hamilton, Executive Director of Operations, and also at Jefferson County School District, Golden, Colorado, by John McDonald, Executive Director of Security and Emergency Planning.

Since its introduction in 2012, other districts and agencies have also contributed.

The Job Action Sheets in this book were inspired by the work of Michelle Brady, Emergency Planning Coordinator, Hillsboro School District, Hillsboro, Oregon.

Other aspects of the Job Action Sheets in this book were inspired by the work of Kevin Sutherland, Emergency Planning Coordinator, Beaverton School District, Beaverton, Oregon.

Other materials were sourced from the phenomenal work of Will Schwall, Emergency Manager, Hays County Sheriff's Office, San Marcos, Texas.

OBJECTIVES

The objective of this manual is to help districts develop, train and mobilize a district reunification team, and implement tangible, on-site and off-site reunification plans. Inherent in this objective is creating or strengthening partnerships with first responder agencies – police, fire and medical. By having district and school personnel build a well designed draft plan, it becomes easier to engage the first responders and other key participants in the planning process. During this process, a core philosophy is essential:

Cops own the crime.
Fire owns the flames.
Schools own the kids.
Paramedics own the patient.

Additionally, performing a successful reunification is much more likely when drills are conducted in advance of an incident. Tabletop exercises and live exercises should be scheduled and performed.

THE PROCESS IN A NUTSHELL

The materials in this manual provide the fundamentals for a comprehensive district plan. The beauty of the Standard Reunification Method is its simplicity.

- Establish a parent check-in location.
- Deliver the students to the student staging area, beyond the field of vision of parents/guardians.
- Once students are on site, notify parents of location.
- "Greeters" direct parents/guardians to the parent check-in location, and help them understand the process.
- Parents/guardians complete Reunification Cards.
- Procedure allows parents/guardians to self-sort during check in, streamlining the process.
- The "Reunifier" recovers student from the student staging area and delivers to the parent.
- Controlled lines of sight allow for an orderly flow, and issues can be handled with diminished drama or anxiety.
- Medical, notification, or investigative contingencies are anticipated.
- Pedestrian "flows" are created so lines don't cross.
- When it's all said and done, successful reunification is about managing the student and parent experience.

WHEN TO INITIATE A REUNIFICATION

Initiating a reunification can be a result of anything abnormal at the school or in the area: power or phone outage, weather event, hazmat incident, bomb threats, criminal activity in the area, or active violence at the school.

In some cases it may be only a partial student population reunification. For instance, criminal activity in the area might result in reunifying students who walk to and from school.

NEAR VAN ARSDALE ELEMENTARY - ARVADA
JEFFCO SHERIFF'S OFFICE REPORTS SHOTS FIRED
FUGITIVE ARRESTED   RIDER KILLED   THEFT SUSPECTS

KEEP PARENTS OUTSIDE

The process works best when you can keep the parents outside of the building. If weather or circumstance dictate parents should be inside the building, give special attention to walking flows and sightlines. Caution tape is a secret "force field" when establishing the parent staging areas within a building.

WHY USE CARDS?

Many schools use electronic rosters or campus information systems. Wouldn't that be easier? The reality is a little different. First and foremost is access to data. Foundation research indicates that in any high profile incident, and even many local ones, internet and cell service become intermittent or even unresponsive. Often school WiFi is impacted as well.

THE CARD

The Reunification Card does a ton of work. Its primary function is to provide accountability, so one student per card is recommended. It also helps with the parent experience. The card is perforated and gives parents a sense of progress as they go through the process.

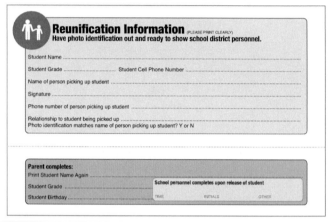

A LITTLE SOCIAL ENGINEERING

A reunification typically occurs because of a crisis or emergency. Consequently, not just students and parents are trying to function at extraordinary stress levels; staff, their families and other first responders also feel the strain. By having a defined process with signage, cards, branding, procedures and protocols, the school presents an organized, calm face to all involved. Fear or uncertainty often results from the unknown. By adopting, communicating and practicing a "known" procedure, the school removes some of that uncertainty.

The cards also bring anxiety down a notch. Asking a parent to complete the form is a familiar activity and will demand the parent slow down and perform a cognitive action, "Here, read the instructions on back, and we'll get things started," might be the first step in lowering parental blood pressure.

INCIDENT COMMAND SYSTEM

Whether it is a man-made or natural crisis, or an act of violence in the school, law enforcement, fire and medical teams will be involved in the school or district's reunification process. Learning to understand and speak a common language as well as being familiar with their procedures is imperative to a successful outcome. With that in mind, district and school safety teams must understand and use the Incident Command System.

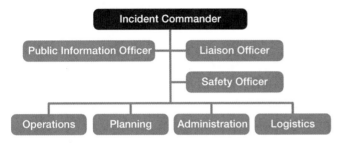

NOT SO WEIRD ADVICE

At first blush, this bit of advice may sound weird to educators: *"Check out FEMA. Go to http://training.fema.gov and complete the online training for IS-100 SCa Introduction to Incident Management for Schools."* The course takes about an hour and a half to complete and introduces some basic emergency response principles in the context of school safety.

Here's why this advice isn't as weird as it sounds. Every first responder agency that partners with schools uses "Incident Command" during a crisis. The "Incident Command System" (ICS) is a response method that determines the role of everyone responding to a crisis and defines a shared vocabulary and shared expectations of behavior.

District and school safety teams need this shared vocabulary when interacting with first responders during a crisis. Equally important is that, when meeting with first responders, having the concepts and vocabulary of Incident Command removes some of the language barriers. It also shows a commitment to success that departments and agencies will appreciate.

PRIORITY, OBJECTIVE, STRATEGY, TACTIC

A valuable FEMA resource is the *Incident Action Planning Guide,* and it's a good start in understanding how first responders manage an incident.

From a school or district perspective, it's important to understand that the incident commander has an expectation that to be useful during the event, the school or district personnel need to have some experience with incident command.

If the school or district personnel don't exhibit any knowledge of the process, their input may be marginalized.

Source: *https://www.fema.gov/media-library/assets/documents/25028*

ARTICULATE YOUR P.O.S.T.

The first step in incident management is defining the priorities, objectives, strategies and tactics that will be used during the event. While every incident will be unique, there are considerations that can be addressed in advance.

Priorities:
- Student and staff safety and well being.
- Student and staff whereabouts and condition.
- Starting the recovery process.

Objectives:
- Every student has been accounted for.
- Every staff member has been accounted for.
- Every student still in the school's control is reunited with their parent or guardian.

Strategies:
- The Standard Reunification Method

Tactics:
- Tactics will vary based on the event and the environment, but look at the typical lifecycles on page 16 for a jumpstart.

JOINT INFORMATION CENTER AND THE SOCIAL MEDIA TEAM

An essential role in the JIC is the Social Media Team. The team should have a couple of people monitoring social media outlets, and when directed by the lead Public Information Officer, releasing any information to social media outlets. Twitter especially seems to have the highest level of activity during an event.

If possible, Public Information Officers (PIO) from all of the responding departments or agencies and the district PIO should be physically together with the Social Media Team. If it's a criminal event, there is a growing trend for law enforcement to assign a detective or investigator to the JIC to monitor social media for evidentiary information.

It is important to recognize that if students have been transported to a separate reunification site, a second command structure will be set up there as well. It may be labeled as a division under Unified Command and will need resources from first responders, but a command structure will need to be established to manage the reunification process, separate from the initial incident.

TWO TEAMS:
TRANSPORT AND REUNIFICATION

With an offsite reunification, the district reunification team will deploy to the reunification site. Other responsibilities need to be managed at the impacted school. Regardless of criminal activity, law enforcement resources will be required.

There are two teams the district must field for an offsite reunification. The team at the impacted school facilitates transport and initiates accountabilty processing.

The reunification team deploys to the reunification site for staging and ultimately student/parent reunification, and return transportation of teachers and staff.

IMPACTED SCHOOL: TRANSPORT TEAM

The team at the impacted school has these priorities:

* Assemble a master student roster, teacher roster and guest roster
* Identify and notify reunification site
* Provide safe transport of students and staff to reunification site
* If there are injuries, additional district personnel assign to the receiving care facilities.

LAW ENFORCEMENT SUPPORT

At the impacted site law enforcement support may be necessary. Some assignments may include:

* Traffic Control
* Crowd Control
* ID Verification
* Perimeter Control
* Security
* Liaison

In the event of criminal activity, LE will typically take the lead in Unified Command.

At the secure assembly area, law enforcement may search students and staff. One important consideration for law enforcement is, if possible, perform the search of students out of sight of the media.

TRANSPORTATION DIRECTOR

Whether the district runs its own buses or service is contracted out, the Transportation Director should be involved in all planning, drilling and training for reunification.

TRANSPORT OPERATIONAL
ROLES AND DUTIES

The following outlines the roles and duties of the Transportation Team. For detailed tasks see the Job Action Sheets.

Transport Incident Commander Coordinate Priorities, Objectives, Strategies and Tactics for an accountable, easy, reunification of students with parents.

Public Information Officer Communicate with parents and press, if appropriate. Coordinate use of mass call or text messages

Social Media Team Monitor social media. Use Twitter to communicate with parents and press, if appropriate.

Safety Officer Observe site and remedy safety concerns.

Liaison Officer Communicate with Fire, Medical or Law Enforcement.

Operations Chief Establish and manage operational staff.

Planning Chief Establish and manage planning staff.

Finance/Administration Chief Establish and manage administrative staff.

Logistics Chief Establish and manage logistical staff.

Student Assembly Director Establish and manage the Student Assembly Area.

Leads For span of control, some roles may need leads.

Victim Advocates/Counselors Standby unless needed.

Kid Wranglers Teachers and Staff who arrive with students remain in the Student Assembly Area to manage students. Additional people may be assigned to this task.

Scribe Document events. A yellow pad is sufficient.

Runner Assist Incident Command if needed.

Transportation Direct transportation needs.

Communications Facilitate radio and other communication needs.

Facilities Coordinate any physical plant needs.

School Principal High priority for transport to the reunification site. Be present at Parent reunification site.

Superintendent Verify reunification site and notification.

TEACHERS: STAY WITH YOUR STUDENTS

Interviews with safety directors directly impacted by crisis reveal a common thread. Often teachers will group together in the immediate aftermath, or assume their job is done when police arrive on scene. It's important to emphasize that teachers should remain with their students and aren't done until all of the students have been reunited with their families. Certainly, exceptions are appropriate for teachers who are also parents of impacted students.

SAMPLE TRANSPORT ORGANIZATION CHART

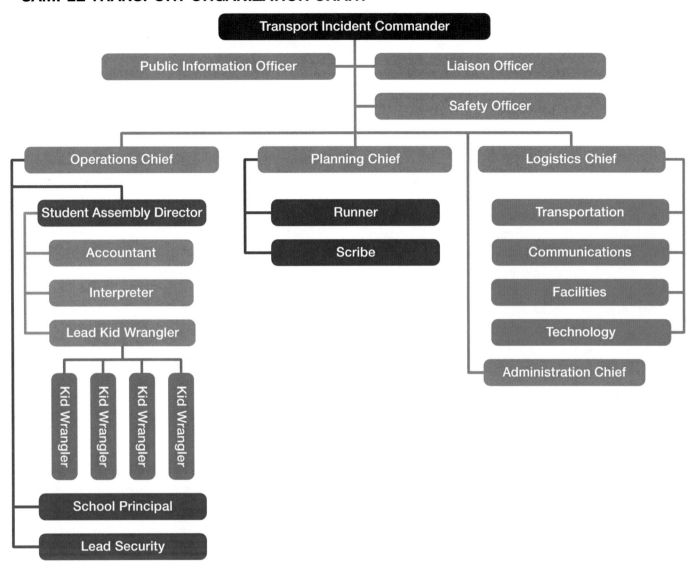

STANDARD™
REUNIFICATION METHOD

THE DISTRICT REUNIFICATION TEAM

Most often the Reunification Team is populated by district personnel. There are several reasons for this:

- Training can be more readily coordinated.
- Experienced teams are more proficient.
- School based teams may initially be unavailable.

Smaller districts may recruit from various schools' administrators in order to populate the team. Extremely small districts may recruit volunteers from the community to staff the Reunification Team. A good rule of thumb for team size is one per hundred students, plus another five members.

Once school staff are at the reunification site, there are roles that the school staff will assume. It's important to train school staff in their role during a reunification.

WHO ARE VICTIM ADVOCATES?

Many law enforcement agencies, district attorneys, and prosecutors have victim advocates on staff and a cadre of volunteers. They often deploy when there is a crisis. Very often they are trained in Psychological First Aid and can be helpful with crisis counseling, if needed, during a reunification. Recruit and train these community partners.

INCLUDING FIRST RESPONDERS

It is absolutely imperative that as the reunification plan is developed, first responders are brought into the process. Meeting with command staff, including PIOs, both law enforcement and Fire/EMS will generate two outcomes. First, they will look at your plan from their perspective. Second, they have suggestions you might not have thought of.

During a Standard Reunification Method workshop, conducted by The Foundation, a fire chief requested the training for every fire station in his city. When questioned why, he replied, "We are going to be on scene. If we're not actively engaged in fire or EMS, we can help with the reunification process."

LAW ENFORCEMENT SUPPORT

At the reunification site law enforcement support may be necessary. Some assignments may include:

- Traffic Control
- Crowd Control
- ID Verification
- Perimeter Control
- Security
- Liaison

OPERATIONAL ROLES AND DUTIES

The following outlines the roles and duties of the Reunification Team. For detailed tasks see the Job Action Sheets.

Reunification Incident Commander Coordinate Priorities, Objectives, Strategies and Tactics for an accountable, easy reunification of students with parents.

Public Information Officer Communicate with parents and press, if appropriate. Coordinate use of mass call or text messages.

Social Media Team Monitor social media. Tweet parents and press, if appropriate.

Safety Officer Observe site and remedy safety concerns.

Liaison Officer Communicate with Fire, Medical or Law Enforcement.

Operations Chief Establish and manage operational staff.

Planning Chief Establish and manage planning staff.

Finance/Administration Chief Establish and manage administrative staff.

Logistics Chief Establish and manage logistical staff.

Parent Check-in Director Establish and manage the check-in process.

Student Assembly Director Establish and manage the Student Assembly Area.

Leads For span of control, some roles may need leads.

Greeters Help coordinate the parent lines. Tell parents about the process. Help verify parents without ID.

Checkers Verify ID and possibly custody rights of parents or guardians. Direct parents to Reunification Area.

Reunifier Take bottom of Reunification Card to Assembly Area, locate student and bring to Reunification Area. Ask student, "Are you okay going home with this person?"

Flow Monitor Observe and remedy process hiccups.

Victim Advocates/Counselors Standby unless needed.

Kid Wranglers Teachers and Staff who arrive with students remain in the Student Assembly Area to manage students. Additional people may be assigned to this task.

Entertainment Director At the elementary level, deploying a projector and screen can reduce student stress. With middle and high school students, consider turning on a television and tuning to local news if appropriate.

Scribe Document events. A yellow pad is sufficient.

Runner Assist Incident Command if needed.

Transportation Directs transportation needs.

Nutrition Services Provide snacks and water.

Communications Facilitate radio and other communication needs.

Facilities Coordinate any physical plant needs.

School Principal Serve as the "Face of the school" at the Reunification Area.

SAMPLE OFFSITE REUNIFICATION ORGANIZATION CHART

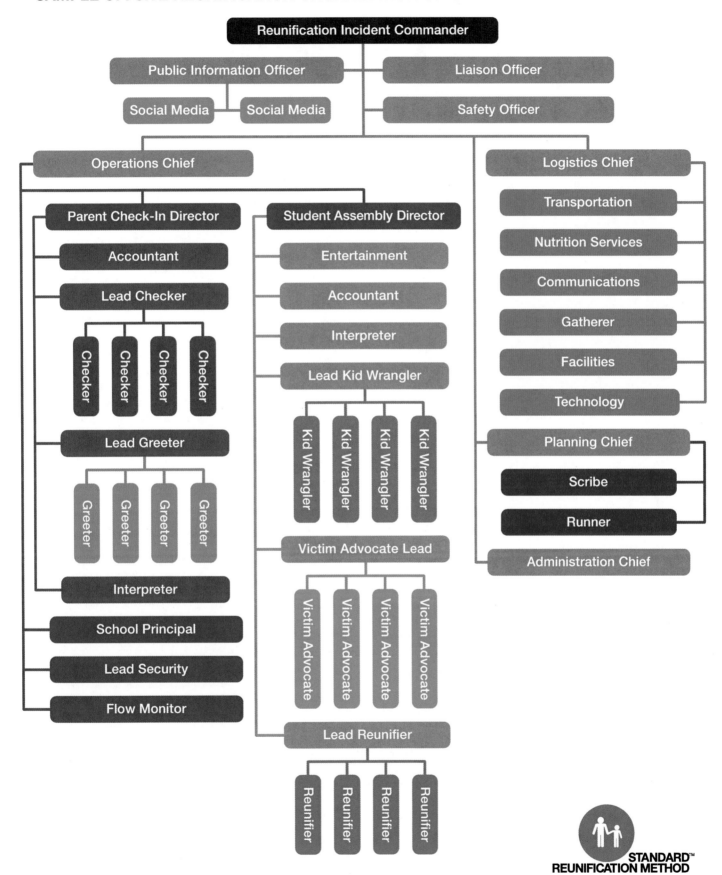

SRP Lifecycle with

EXAMPLE 1: SECURE

Scenario: Criminal activity in the area has resulted in the school going into Secure. Students were brought into the building. Business as usual inside, but no one is let in or out.

Law enforcement has indicated that a normal release of the students can occur, but the situation outside isn't resolved.

Considerations: With criminal activity in area of the school, it's decided that students who walk home should have their parents pick them up.

Reunification Incident Command: Because there was no criminal or safety issue in the school, Reunification Incident Command would be led by the school safety team. Coordination with Law Enforcement Incident Command of the criminal activity would be needed.

Public Information Officer: Because the school was not directly involved in criminal activity, the school or district would lead public information within the school community. District PIO would inform LE PIO of the media messaging.

Notifications: Depending on the situation, parents and media may be notified that the school has been placed in Secure. Additional notification will be made to parents who would need to pick up their students.

Police Role in Reunification: With criminal activity in the area, but not directly near the school, officers may be asked to assist with reunification. Some duties might include assisting with parent identification (for the parents without ID), traffic control, or simply uniformed presence. Patrol resources may also be relocated near the school.

SECURE LIFECYCLE
- School is placed in Secure.
- Parents are notified.
- Business goes as usual within the school.
- Law enforcement presence around the school is increased
- The Standard Reunification Method is utilized for the students that walk home at the end of school day.

EXAMPLE 2: LOCKDOWN

Scenario: At the middle school, an armed intruder is seen in the building. Students and staff immediately lock classroom doors, turn out the lights, and remain out of sight. Law enforcement arrives on scene.

Considerations: Because it is still an active law enforcement response and investigation, the decision is made to transport the students to a nearby community center for reunification.

Unified Command: Because it is an active crime scene, law enforcement would lead Unified Command at the middle school site.

Reunification Incident Command: At the reunification site, a command structure is established to manage the reunification.

Joint Information Center: Because it is an active crime scene, the law enforcement PIO would be the primary press representative. The school or district PIO would be in the JIC, communicating with the PIO at the reunification site.

Notifications: Parents and media are notified that the school has been placed in Lockdown. Additional notifications are made to parents on the location of the reunification site once students are in route or at the site.

Police Role in Reunification: While the school has become an active crime scene, some officers will be assigned to the reunification site. Depending on the site, police may decide to sweep the area prior to students arriving. In addition to the duties outlined in the Secure example, detectives may be on scene for witness interviews and statements.

LOCKDOWN LIFECYCLE
- School is placed in Lockdown.
- Multiple law enforcement agencies arrive on scene.
- Students and staff are evacuated classroom by classroom to the Secure Assembly Area. In this case, the gym is secured by law enforcement.
- Parents begin to arrive outside of the police perimeter.
- The media arrive on scene.
- Internet, WiFi, and cell services become intermittent or unresponsive.
- Police secure the reunification site.
- District mobilizes Reunification Team.
- Buses are deployed and students are transported to the reunification site.
- Parents are notified of location.
- The Standard Reunification Method is utilized.

Reunification

EXAMPLE 3: EVACUTE

Scenario: An unknown cause has resulted in thick smoke in the middle school. Students successfully evacuate to the football field.

Considerations: Because it is still an active fire response and investigation, the decision is made to transport the students to a nearby high school for reunification.

Unified Command: Because it is an active fire event, the fire department would lead Unified Command at the middle school site.

Reunification Incident Command: At the reunification site, a command structure is established to manage the reunification.

Joint Information Center: Because it is an active fire event, the fire department PIO would be the primary press representative. The school or district PIO would be in the JIC, communicating with the PIO at the reunification site.

Notifications: Parents and media are notified that the school has been evacuated. Additional notifications are made to parents on the location of the reunification site once students are in route or at the site.

Police Role in Reunification: While the school is an active fire scene, the school requests assistance from law enforcement. Officers are assigned to the reunification site.

EVACUATE LIFECYCLE
- Parents begin to arrive outside of the perimeter.
- The media arrive on scene.
- Internet, WiFi, and cell services are intermittent or unresponsive.
- Police secure the reunification site.
- District mobilizes Reunification Team.
- Buses are deployed and students are transported to the reunification site.
- Parents are notified of site location.
- The Standard Reunification Method is utilized.

EXAMPLE 4: SHELTER

Scenario: A nearby wildland fire has resulted in mandatory neighborhood evacuations. The Red Cross is requesting the high school as a designated shelter.

Considerations: Due to the community value of the high school as a Red Cross shelter, the decision is made to accept the request. With area residents arriving, and bus routes affected, the decision is made to transport students to a school outside of the impacted area.

Unified Command: Because it is an active fire event, the fire department would lead Unified Command, but shelter is only one aspect. The Red Cross would establish their command structure division at the shelter high school.

Reunification Incident Command: At the reunification site, a command structure is established to manage the reunification.

Joint Information Center: Because it is a large scale event, managed by Unified Command, the most experienced PIO would be the primary press representative. The school or district PIO would be in the JIC, communicating with the PIO at the reunification site.

Notifications: Parents and media are notified that the school has been evacuated. Additional notifications are made to parents on the location of the reunification site once students are in route or at the site.

Police Role in Reunification: The school which is the reunification site requests assistance from law enforcement. Officers are assigned to the reunification site.

SHELTER LIFECYCLE
- Parents begin to arrive outside of the perimeter.
- The media arrive on scene.
- Internet, WiFi, and cell services are intermittent or unresponsive.
- Police secure the reunification site.
- District mobilizes Reunification Team.
- Buses are deployed and students are transported to the reunification site.
- Parents are notified of site location.
- The Standard Reunification Method is utilized.

SRM Staging the

STEP 1
ESTABLISH ONSITE INCIDENT COMMAND

The first step in staging for transport is establishing School Incident Command at the affected school. Integrating with Unified Command should be a priority.

Priorities: Student and staff safety and wellbeing
Student and staff whereabouts and condition
Assemble affected school command staff
Integrate with Unified Command
Joint Information Center established

Objectives: Safe transport of students and staff to reunification site

Strategy: The Standard Reunification Method

Tactics: Will be determined by the environment

STEP 2
CLASSROOM EVACUATION

Classrooms are individually evacuated to the Secure Assembly Area. During a Police Led Evacuation, students and staff will be asked to keep their hands visible.

If it is a Police Led Evacuation after a Lockdown, each room will be cleared by Law Enforcement personnel. This process may take up to several hours. Teacher should take attendance in the classroom, prior to evacuation.

SPECIAL NEEDS POPULATIONS

The Individuals with Disabilities Act mandates additional supports for students with special education needs in school setting. These supports would also function to provide supervision and assistance to students with disabilities during emergency situations.

SRM Actions and

COMMUNITY ACTION
PARENTS WILL BEGIN TO ARRIVE

Parents will be arriving at the impacted school. Often with a Lockdown event, adjoining schools will go into Lockout. Parents may be arriving at those schools as well.

REUNIFICATION SITE
MOBILIZE REUNIFICATION TEAM

Contacting the Superintendent and determining the Reunification Site are among the first actions taken. If the site is another school, early release may be necessary.

School for Transport

STEP 3
SECURE ASSEMBLY AREA

At the Secure Assembly Area it is preferable that teachers stay with their students. If some teachers are unable to be at the Secure Assembly Area, doubling up classes with "Partner" teachers is appropriate.

STEP 4
STUDENT AND STAFF TRANSPORT

Students and staff board the bus and are transported to the Reunification Site. Buses having audio video systems can be utilized for further accountability by having students face the camera and state their name.

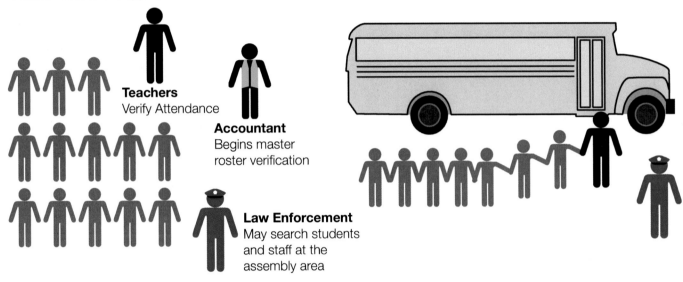

Teachers
Verify Attendance

Accountant
Begins master roster verification

Law Enforcement
May search students and staff at the assembly area

Considerations

LAW ENFORCEMENT
SUPPORT AND INVESTIGATIONS

Regardless of criminal activity, law enforcement support will be necessary at both the impacted school and the reunification site.

FIRE AND EMS
CASUALTY CARE

If necessary, Fire and EMS will establish Casualty Collection, Triage and Transport areas. Many fire departments are also willing to assist in the transport and reunification process, if they are not actively responding to crisis.

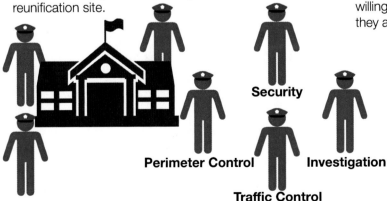

Security

Perimeter Control

Investigation

Traffic Control

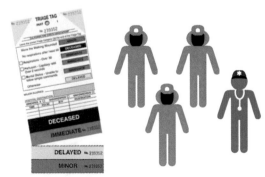

SRM Staging the

ASSEMBLY AREA
STUDENTS ENTER OUT OF PARENTAL VIEW

Students are transported to the Reunification Site and are then directed to the Student Assembly Area. Often this is a cafeteria or gymnasium. Upon arrival, students are verified against a master roster.

It is important that students are not in view of their parents when exiting the bus and entering the reunification site.

GREETING AREA
PARENTS ARE MET HERE

As parents arrive, signage directs them to Parent Check-in Table. Greeters begin the process by asking parents to complete the Reunification Card.

Law Enforcement
Often an Officer is posted where students are disembarking.

LE

Student Check-in Table

Law Enforcement Interviews

Student Assembly Area

Transport Students to Site

Helpful Tip
As parents wait for reunification with their student, try to have them clustered rather than in a line. Students may not always be recovered in the order parents line up.

Law Enforcement
Often an Officer is posted where parents wait for reunification.

LE

Parent Reunification Area

Reunification Site

CHECK-IN TABLE
SET UP MULTIPLE LINES
Establish parallel check-in lines based on first initial of last name. Checkers verify ID and custody.

REUNIFICATION AREA
PARENT STUDENT REUNIFICATION
As their tasks are completed, Greeters and Checkers can be reassigned as Reunifiers.

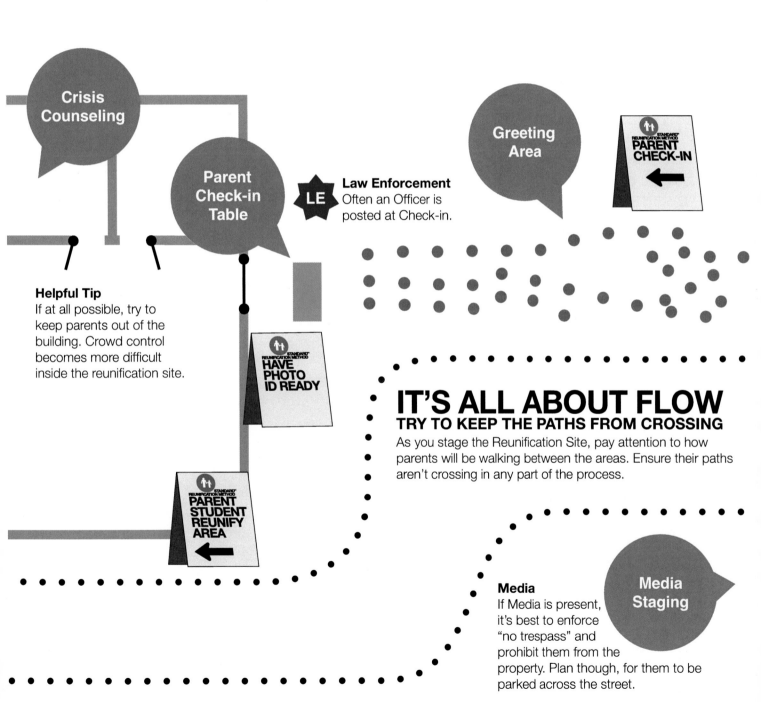

Crisis Counseling

Parent Check-in Table

LE **Law Enforcement**
Often an Officer is posted at Check-in.

Greeting Area

STANDARD REUNIFICATION METHOD
PARENT CHECK-IN ←

Helpful Tip
If at all possible, try to keep parents out of the building. Crowd control becomes more difficult inside the reunification site.

STANDARD REUNIFICATION METHOD
HAVE PHOTO ID READY

STANDARD REUNIFICATION METHOD
PARENT STUDENT REUNIFY AREA ←

IT'S ALL ABOUT FLOW
TRY TO KEEP THE PATHS FROM CROSSING
As you stage the Reunification Site, pay attention to how parents will be walking between the areas. Ensure their paths aren't crossing in any part of the process.

Media
If Media is present, it's best to enforce "no trespass" and prohibit them from the property. Plan though, for them to be parked across the street.

Media Staging

SRM The Process

STEP 1
GREETINGS
As parents arrive at the reunification site, Greeters explain the process and distribute Reunification Cards.

STEP 2
PARENTS FILL OUT CARD
Parents complete the information requested on the card, and begin to self-sort into lines.

STEP 3
CHECKERS VERIFY ID
Parent custody is verified. The card is torn on the perforation and the bottom is returned to the parent. The top is given to the Accountant.

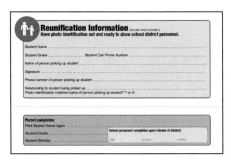

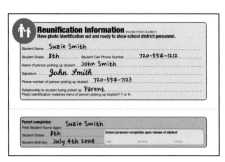

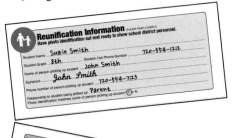

Greeter
Greeters manage the initial intake of parents, explaining the process and answering questions that may arise.

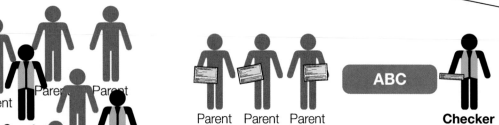

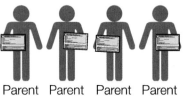

Accountant
The Accountant verifies cards against a master roster and may start sorting cards.

Law Enforcement
A uniformed officer can help with crowd control and identity verification.

Checker
Checkers verify identification. In some cases custodial authority may need verification as well.

in 6 Easy Steps

STEP 4
REUNIFICATION AREA
At the Reunification Area, parents give the bottom of the card to a Reunifier. The Reunifier goes to the Assembly area to get the student.

STEP 5
STUDENT REUNIFICATION
The Reunifier returns the student to their parents asking the student if they feel comfortable leaving with that adult. They then note the time and initial the bottom of the card.

STEP 6
ACCOUNTABILITY
The Reunifier delivers the bottom of the card to the Student Assembly Accountant. The Accountant may start sorting the cards.

Parent Parent Parent **Reunifier** ● ● ● **Reunifier** ● ● ● **Reunifier**   Parent ● ● ● **Reunifier Accountant**

Principal
It may be beneficial to have the school principal in the area where students and parents are reunified.

WHAT IF?
THE STUDENT ISN'T THERE
If the student isn't in the Assembly Area, the Reunifier hands the card to a Victim Advocate/Crisis Counselor.

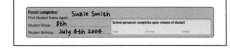

SEPARATE
PARENT FROM THE LINE
The Victim Advocate/Crisis Counselor then separates the parent from the other parents in line and takes them to a private location.

Law Enforcement
A uniformed officer can help with crowd control and keep the peace.

Reunifier ● ● ● **Counselor** ● ● ● **Counselor**

Parent Parent Parent Parent

SRM The Card

REUNIFICATION INFORMATION CARDS

The Standard Reunification Method was created to manage not just the students, but the parental experience of reunification as well. The Reunification Card is an essential element of the method.

Some might initially protest, "What! More Paperwork?" And the answer is "Yes. Precisely." Beyond providing a mechanism for accountability, the card demonstrates to parents that there is a process for this. It shows that school or district has a plan and a method.

The psychology behind the process begins to offer the parent some measure of order in what might be a stressfull time. Filling the card out, then separating the top from the bottom, handing the card to the Reunifier, gives the parent feedback, demonstrating progress in the process. The bottom of the card also provides proxy identification for the parent, removing the need to ID them at every phase.

SEND IT HOME IN ADVANCE?

The question often comes up on whether the school should send the cards home in advance and request parents fill out and return them. Certainly an option, but it creates unneccesary work in collecting the cards and diminishes the parent experience. One alternative is to send the cards home, with the handout, and ask parents to complete the card and put it in their car. This gives parents an expectation of the process and some parents will complete the request. The handout is available on the website and is also reprinted on page 28 of this book.

AVAILABLE IN SPANISH

The Reunification Card is also available in Spanish. Check the website for new translations.

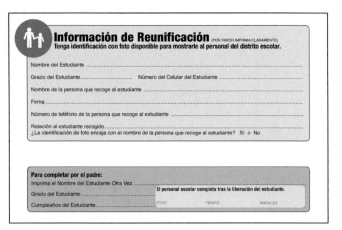

PRESS READY ARTWORK

The Reunification Cards are press ready for your printer. The artwork is set up for *Work and Tumble*[1] on 8½" x 11" index card stock. Ask your printer for a strong perforation. There is little worse than a "bad perf" on reunification day.

[1] *"In prepress and printing, an imposition or layout in which one plate contains all the images (pages) to be printed on both sides of a sheet. When one side of a job has been printed, the pile of printed sheets is turned over, the edge of the sheet that was the gripper edge for the first side becoming the back edge for the second side. After printing, the sheet is cut in half, yielding two identical units."*

Source: *PrintWiki – the Free Encyclopedia of Print. http://printwiki.org*

Reunification Information (PLEASE PRINT CLEARLY)
Have photo identification out and ready to show school district personnel.

Student Name ....

Student Grade .... Student Cell Phone Number ....

Name of person picking up student ....

Signature ....

Phone number of person picking up student ....

Relationship to student being picked up ....
Photo identification matches name of person picking up student? Y or N

Parent completes:

Print Student Name Again ....

Student Grade ....

Student Birthday ....

School personnel completes upon release of student

TIME	INITIALS	OTHER

Parent Guardian Sign Off

I have read and understand these instructions.

Print Your Name .... Date ....

Signature ....

Reunification

First, we want to thank you for your patience during this reunification. We share the same goal during this process: Getting you and your student back together as quickly as possible. The reason we're going through this is that an event has occurred at the school that mandates the school personally reunite you with your child.

Instructions

1. Please complete the information on the other side of this card.
2. Prepare identification (If you don't have ID with you, please move to the side of the line, it may take a little longer to verify your identity.)
3. Select the check-in line based on either student last name or student grade.
4. After check-in, staff will split this card and a runner will be sent to recover your student. Please step over to the Reunification Location.
5. If there has been injury or other concerns, you may be asked to meet a counselor.
6. Please don't shout at school or district staff. We'll get through this as quickly as possible.

STANDARD™ REUNIFICATION METHOD

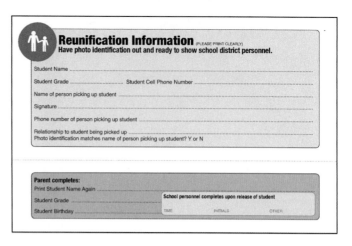

Reunification Information (PLEASE PRINT CLEARLY)
Have photo identification out and ready to show school district personnel.

Student Name ....

Student Grade .... Student Cell Phone Number ....

Name of person picking up student ....

Signature ....

Phone number of person picking up student ....

Relationship to student being picked up ....
Photo identification matches name of person picking up student? Y or N

Parent completes:
Print Student Name Again ....

Student Grade ....

Student Birthday ....

School personnel completes upon release of student

TIME   INITIALS   OTHER

STUDENT/PARENT REUNIFICATION
Circumstances may occur at the school that require parents to pick up their students in a formalized, controlled release. This process is called a Reunification and may be necessary due to weather, a power outage, hazmat or if a crisis occurs at the school. The Standard Reunification Method is a protocol that makes this process more predictable and less chaotic for all involved.

Because a reunification is not a typical end of school day event, a reunification may occur at a different location than the school a student attends. If this location is another school, then those students may be subject to a controlled release as well.

NOTIFICATION
Parents may be notified in a number of ways. The school or district may use its broadcast phone or text message system. In some cases, students may be asked to send a text message to their parents. A reunification text message from a student may look something like this: *"The school has closed, please pick me up at 3:25 at the main entrance. Bring your ID. "*

PARENT/GUARDIAN EXPECTATIONS
If a parent or guardian is notified that a reunification is needed, there are some expectations that parents or guardians should be aware of. First, bring identification. That will streamline things during reunification. Second, be patient. Reunification is a process that protects both the safety of the student and provides for an accountable change of custody from the school to a recognized custodial parent or guardian.

WHAT IF A PARENT CAN'T PICK-UP THEIR STUDENT?
When a parent can't immediately go to the reunification site, students will only be released to individuals previously identified as a student's emergency contact. Otherwise, the school will hold students until parents can pick up their student.

WHAT IF THE STUDENT DROVE TO SCHOOL?
There may be instances where a student may not be allowed to remove a vehicle from the parking lot. In this case, parents are advised to recover the student. In some circumstances, high school students may be released on their own.

HOW IT WORKS
For students, the school asks that students be orderly and quiet while waiting. Students may be asked to text a message to their parents or guardians. Students are also asked not to send other text messages either in or out of the school or reunification area. Keeping the cellular network usage at a minimum may be important during a reunification.

REUNIFICATION CARDS
For parents, there are a couple of steps. If a parent is driving to the school, greater awareness of traffic and emergency vehicles is advised. Parents should park where indicated and not abandon vehicles. Parents are asked to go to the Reunification "Check In" area and form lines based on the first letter of their student's last name. While in line, parents are asked to fill out a reunification card. This card is perforated and will be separated during the process. Some of the same information is repeated on both the top and separated bottom of the card. Parents are asked to complete all parts of the card.

In the case of multiple students being reunified, a separate card for each student needs to be completed.

BRING ID TO CHECK IN
During check in, identification and custody rights are confirmed. The card is separated and the bottom half given back to the parent.

From the "Check In" area parents are directed to the "Reunification" area. There, a runner will take the bottom half of the card and take it to the Student Assembly Area to recover the student or students.

Parents should be aware that in some cases, they may be invited into the building for further information.

INTERVIEWS AND COUNSELING
In some cases, parents may be advised that a law enforcement investigation is underway and may be advised that interviews are necessary. In extreme cases, parents may be pulled aside for emergency or medical information.

SRM Signage

READY TO PRINT SIGNAGE
Available on the website are downloadable signs. These are sized at 24" x 32" comfortably fitting in most sandwich board curb sign frames.

SRM Planning

GETTING STARTED

Planning for a reunification involves creating documents geared toward a number of audiences. There is a District plan, individual school plans, and plans for first responders.

As with any school safety plan, the concept of plan evolution is ever-present. Events may occur or lessons may be learned that impact these roles or procedures. Emergency planners should also remain vigilant and familiarize themselves with emerging trends regarding school safety and crisis response management in particular.

Additionally, depending on the type of event, plans may suggest Districts ask law enforcement to help evaluate and secure evacuation locations prior to moving students.

THE DISTRICT REUNIFICATION PLAN HAS THE FOLLOWING COMPONENTS:
- Introduction
- Objectives
- Planning team acknowledgment and contact information
- Definitions
- Contact information
- Incident Command structure
- Attendance procedures
- Local site floor plan
- Primary walking evacuation site floor plan
- Primary walking evacuation routes with emergency services routes
- Secondary walking evacuation site floor plan
- Secondary walking evacuation routes with emergency services routes
- Transport plan
- Primary bus evacuation site floor plan
- Primary bus evacuation routes
- School, district, law enforcement, fire, medical, legal and insurance acknowledgment sign-offs
- Emergency services routes
- Secondary bus evacuation site floor plan
- Secondary bus evacuation routes with emergency services routes
- (Optional tertiary bus site information)
- District/School "go kits"
- Notification procedures
- Media management
- Time of day contingencies
- Type of incident contingencies
- Reunification Setup roles and procedures
- Reunification Process roles and procedures
- Reunification Teardown roles and procedures
- Debriefing guidance
- Exercise schedule
- Special needs considerations
- Memorandums of Understanding

FLOOR PLANS AND SITE MAPS

It's important to include on- and off-site floor plans in the reunification plan. If the off-site evacuation location is another school, it's usually a reciprocal case. Given that condition, advance communication and distributed effort can result in both schools having each other's floor plans.

There may be different versions of the floor plan for each reunification location.

- A floor plan with no annotation
- A floor plan annotating student locations during an on-site reunification
- A floor plan annotating both home and guest student locations during an off-site reunification. Occupancy limits should be noted on all rooms used during an off-site reunification.
- A floor plan annotating occupancy in the case of an off-site location not being a school
- A site map with traffic responsibilities
- A site map with the locations of students, check-in and reunification

In the event of criminal activity, witness interview rooms and crisis counselor rooms should be annotated.

In the event of law enforcement debriefing needs, it is strongly suggested that a separate facility be used. While it may initially appear expeditious to conduct law enforcement or SWAT debriefings at the reunification location, further consideration may reveal that recovery of all participants may be impacted by co-mingling first responders and civilians.

EVACUATION ROUTES

In mapping both walking and bus evacuation routes, it's important to identify potential traffic issues and first responder ingress and egress paths. The routes from the nearest fire station and the routes to the nearest hospitals must be considered. Are walking paths crossing streets that will be used by first responders? Are there some predictable streets that would be common for parents to use?

SEXUAL OFFENDERS

It is also beneficial to determine the nature of the neighborhood around schools or other evacuation sites. Most states provide a mapping utility to locate sexual offenders. These maps often link to a database that provides name, address and photo of the convicted felon. It is important to identify these individuals and their proximity to the site. There are many documented cases of sexual predators using a crisis as an opportunity for sexual predation.

ROUTE MAP CHECKLIST

These considerations should be included when mapping routes:

- Evacuation routes
- Incident Command Post locations
- Incoming district responder routes
- Incoming fire routes
- Incoming medical routes
- Outgoing medical routes
- Incoming parent routes
- Outgoing parent routes
- Staging area
- Landing zone
- Media staging
- Reunification signage locations
- Parent check-in location
- Possible road block sites
- Possible neighborhood evacuation perimeter
- Sexual offender locations
- Security perimeter
- Long perimeter

NOTIFICATION PROCEDURES

In the event of a reunification, parent/guardian notification is a necessary first step. Many schools or districts have mass notification systems to bulk call and/or text information to the parent population. It is imperative that accurate, factual information be delivered, starting with the crucial First Message. While it may seem comforting to tell parents that everyone is okay, or to minimize the number of injuries, this First Message not only begins the recovery process, it may be evidentiary for purposes of liability. Rather than saying "All students are safe," it is probably more accurate to report that, "We are in the process of establishing the safety status of all students and staff."

With the number of cell phones available to ever younger student populations, parents will, in all likelihood, be the first to arrive at the impacted school. Prepare for the fact that this may occur prior to the transmission of any official notification by the school or the district.

Students will call or text their parents/guardians immediately during a crisis, despite school policy prohibiting mobile phone use. Additionally, some schools may not have accurate contact information for all parents. It may be possible during a crisis to leverage this to the school's advantage by writing out reunification information for the students to text to their parents/guardians.

Prepared notification language is vital. While anything written in advance may not exactly fit the circumstances of any given crisis, it may provide a valuable advantage in the initial phase of a crisis. These statements can be vetted with the district public information officer and legal counsel as part of the planning process. Other notifications should be considered. Contacting district legal counsel, as well as the district's insurance providers, should be part of the notification process.

SPECIAL NEEDS CONSIDERATIONS

Schools are encouraging parents of students with special medication needs to consult their physicians about medication Go Kits. The medication Go Kit may include extra dosages that are not in the school medicine locker. If it's determined that the school does create a medication Go Kit, security and chain of custody should be part of the plan and procedure.

The Individuals with Disabilities Act mandates additional supports for students with special education needs in school setting. These supports would also function to provide supervision and assistance to students with disabilities during emergency situations.

TIME OF DAY CONTINGENCIES

Time of day may impact how a reunification evolves. A crisis at the end of the day, when buses are already on site, may actually require a controlled release reunification. It is not beneficial to immediately release students who have witnessed a traumatic incident, even though the buses are there and it's the end of the school day. Mental health concerns might dictate a controlled release so that crisis counseling can be made available. This mandates a site plan that includes bus staging areas.

PARENTS ARE CAPABLE

There may be circumstances where some of the early arrival parents can be given a task. This is situational, but consider that, when given a job, parents are now helping with the crisis. This has important psychological benefits in addition to distributing labor. "Can you help set up this table?" or "Could you help me by placing these signs along Elm street?" Both are necessary tasks, and can enlist the parent into being part of the solution.

GO KITS FOR REUNIFICATION

Reunification Go Kits contain specialized items that are unique to the reunification process, such as caution tape, clip boards and pens, signage, and reunification cards). Consequently, these kits are different than school evacuation Go Kits. Since reunification is often managed by District personnel, reunification Go Kits aren't necessary at each school, rather the kits can stay with District response teams. Larger districts may have several kits, one at the district office and others in the trunks or backs of vehicles used by District responders. Smaller Districts may have only two kits. One at the District office, and one with the primary District responder. (Two is a suggested minimum: redundancy is important.) Inventories and locations should be audited once a quarter.

THE RUNIFICATION OPERATION KIT

Available on the website are templates to create a Runification Operation Kit.

FAQs

FREQUENTLY ASKED QUESTIONS

Since introducing the Standard Reunification Method in 2012, thousands of districts, departments and agencies have scrutinized, evaluated and ultimately implemented the program. During the process some questions seem to come up often.

SERIOUSLY, WHAT DOES IT REALLY COST?

Since its introduction in 2009, public K12 schools, districts, departments and agencies were free to use The "I Love U Guys" Foundation programs at no cost.

In 2015, the Foundation expanded availability, and now offers the programs to any public or private organization at no charge. Simply download the materials and begin the process.

DO WE NEED TO BUY TRAINING IN ORDER TO USE THE PROGRAMS?

No. We've attempted to put enough material online so that schools and law enforcement can successfully implement Foundation programs. We know of thousands of schools across the US and Canada that have implemented the programs using internal resources.

That said, part of our sustainability model relies not just on charitable giving, but in providing training for districts departments and agencies. If your organization is interested in Foundation training, please contact us for rates and terms.

CAN I MODIFY MATERIALS?

Some details may need to be customized to your location. For instance, the classroom poster should be modified to include hazards and safety strategies that are specific to your location.

ARE THE SOURCE MATERIALS AVAILABLE?

Yes. Some of the materials are available. Original, digital artwork can be provided to organizations that have signed a "Notice of Intent" or a "Memorandum of Understanding" with The "I Love U Guys" Foundation.

Please note: Currently, we are migrating from Pages on the Mac to QuarkXPress. (Adobe InDesign made our eyes bleed. Depending on the material original artwork is only provided in Mac OS X, Pages version 4.3 iWork '09.

CAN YOU SEND ME MATERIALS IN MICROSOFT WORD?

With the exception of the Runification Operation Kit, no. Retaining the graphic integrity of the materials proved beyond our capabilities using Microsoft Word.

CAN I REALLY USE THE MATERIALS? WHAT ABOUT COPYRIGHTS AND TRADEMARKS?

Schools, districts, departments, agencies and organizations are free to use the materials under the "Terms of Use" outlined in this document.

DO I NEED TO ASK PERMISSION TO USE THE MATERIALS?

No. You really don't need to ask permission. But, it would be fabulous if you let us know that you're using our programs.

DO I HAVE TO SIGN AN MOU WITH THE FOUNDATION?

It is not necessary to sign an MOU with the Foundation. But, please consider it. The Foundation is committed to providing programs at no cost. Yet, program development, enhancement and support are cost centers for us. One way we fund those costs is through private grants and funding.

An MOU is a strong demonstration of program validity and assists us with these types of funding requests.

DO I HAVE TO SEND A NOTICE OF INTENT?

In the absence of an MOU, a Notice of Intent provides similar value to us regarding demonstrations of program validity to potential funders.

DO I HAVE TO NOTIFY YOU AT ALL THAT I AM USING THE SRM?

We often speak with school safety stakeholders that have implemented the SRM but hadn't quite mentioned it to us. Please, please, please let us know that your school, district, department or agency is using the SRP.

It is our goal that the SRP becomes the "Gold Standard." The more schools, districts, departments and agencies that we can show are using the program, the greater the chance for achieving our goal.

CAN I PUT OUR LOGO ON YOUR MATERIALS?

Yes. But with some caveats. If you are a school, district, department or agency you may include your logo on posters and handouts. If you are a commercial enterprise, please contact us in advance with intended usage.

In some states we have co-branding agreements with "umbrella" organizations. In those states we ask that you also include the umbrella organizations branding.

Please see http://iloveuguys.org/cobranding for a list of current states and organizations.

WE WOULD LIKE TO PUT THE MATERIALS ON OUR WEBSITE.

Communication with your community is important. While you are free to place any material on your website, it's preferable that you link to the materials from our website. The reason for this is to allow us to track material usage. We can then use these numbers when we seek funding.

But, don't let that be a show stopper. If your IT group prefers, just copy the materials to your site.

Made in the USA
Monee, IL
17 May 2023

33369782R00021